At Risk

The lives some children live

Diana Cant

At Risk

© Diana Cant

First Edition 2021

Diana Cant has asserted her authorship and given her permission to
Dempsey & Windle for these poems to be published here.

Published by Dempsey & Windle

15 Rosetrees
Guildford
Surrey
GU1 2HS
UK
01483 571164
dempseyandwindle.com

British Library Cataloguing-in-Publication Data

A catalogue record for this book is available from the British Library

ISBN: 978-1-913329-57-0

Printed and bound in the UK

The author is donating all profits from the sale of this book to
the UK children's mental health charity NSPCC
(https://www.nspcc.org.uk)

For John

Contents

An Introduction

These poems are dedicated to all those young people who have had the courage to share so much of themselves and their lives. As a child psychotherapist, working with some of the most deprived and abused young people in our society, I have been profoundly moved by their bravery, resilience and determination to face some early-life experiences many of us cannot imagine, even should we wish to.

The current pandemic and lockdown has made us all acutely aware of the importance and the fragility of our children's mental health. Isolation and uncertainty severely challenge healthy emotional development, and the truly alarming rise in self-harm and suicidal ideation clearly flag this up. As we learn more about the long-term effects of the pandemic, this needs our urgent and creative attention. I have included some relevant statistics as footnotes to some of these poems, to offer a factual context to the often harrowing stories here. To preserve their confidentiality, the children's individual identities have been disguised, and sometimes conflated, but with care not to lose the veracity of their experiences.

One of the things I have learnt from my years of doing this work is to be patient – to listen and to wait, and to do both of those things with an active thoughtfulness. How I listen often matters more than what I say. I have also learnt how long it can take a child to really know what has happened to them. And because that truth, once known, can never be forgotten, my task is to help them find a place within themselves where it can be held in a safer and less damaging way.

These pages contain stories and voices too rarely heard – the voices of young people who have become accustomed to adults making decisions about their lives with little seeming consultation with them. The poems are a small attempt to represent those lives and the courage it takes to live them.

5

"You must be very patient", replied the fox. "First you will sit down at a little distance from me – like that – in the grass. I shall look at you out of the corner of my eye, and you will say nothing. Words are the source of misunderstandings. But you will sit a little closer to me every day…"

Antoine de Saint Exupery (*The Little Prince*)

Archaeology of Loss

We are excavating bones
sunken in the hot, dry ground
where bodies are not often disinterred
but left to disappear.

We must go gently
for every sinew sings of pain
and every tendon tenses
to the pulse of blood long stilled.

As we lift each one,
brush away the grit, we note
the nick, the bulge, the indentation,
the very boneness of the bone.

We raise a femur filled with longing,
a tibia of loneliness
and a scapula, large and flat,
evidence of love from long ago.

We free each one and lay them
bare and gleaming in hallowed ground,
near the river where the warblers hide
and the lush bulrushes grow.

Mouth Organ

This is the morning she sits on the table
drumming a rhythm with her heels
on the cupboard below.

I long to be elsewhere

Brown hair across her eyes, pink socks
floral leggings and a jumper
with a picture of a kitten.

drifting through white space

She glares disdainfully
at the toys on the shelf
and reaches for none of them

turn away from desire

This is the morning she begins
to talk about her life.
Her talk is made of fragments of fear.

suspended in time

She is blind-walking towards
a truth made more bearable
by the absence of nailing words of knowing.

disconnected

She reaches for a mouth organ
and begins to play a keening song
of what might have been but never was.

sadness streams from my lips

At Risk

Because I didn't know he was a paedo, right,
he was just my uncles' mate,
because he used to come round and we'd chat
nothing sexy, just friendly really,
because that gym instructor took me out
and got me drunk
and he knew I was only fifteen,
because he took me to his place
and I woke up in the morning still drunk
and he was having sex with me,
because my mum was furious
said it was rape but only his word against mine
and she grounded me, right,
because I messaged my uncle's mate and said
I might need him to sort someone out for me,
because then the police are at my school
Are you aware that he's a known sex offender?
on the sex register or some such,
because my mum's mad again
won't let me stay home alone
when she's working nights
and I have to go to my dad's,
because he called me a slut
said I'd just end up on my back
giving blowjobs when I grow up,
because my period's late
and it's all a mess
I dunno what to do.

*The commonly called 'At Risk Register' is now known as a Child
Protection Plan. A child can be made subject to a CPP when they
are at risk of suffering significant harm, either physically,
emotionally, by sexual abuse, or by physical or emotional neglect.*

The Art of Disappearance

The tic-tic of her crutches
on the path – she lurches in,
throws her young body
on the consulting room couch,
pulling her rebellious legs after her.

Her body is the theatre
of a many-frontiered war,
her parents' battles etched
deep beneath her flesh before
she put her body armour on.

She stopped eating, started
to control what she could.
So thin she nearly died
yet all she speaks of is food
or no food: thin gruel indeed.

The first time we met, a shrew
ran across the floor between us.
Tiny, delicate, bewildered
it paused mid-flight and sat upright
beady in the reverberating air.

A shrew can dislocate its body
escape into the smallest of spaces
and this it did, disappearing
through a fissure
into the world beyond.

Hospital admissions for eating disorders rose by 37% between 2018/19. Most eating disorders develop during adolescence, and anorexia nervosa has the highest mortality rate of any adolescent psychiatric disorder. Approximately only 60% of those treated make a full recovery. (NHS Digital; 2020)

Forensic

She places the soft mass
on the dissecting table,
dispassionate
as she directs her scalpel
to the gently pulsing problem,
she probes
prepares a transverse section
examines microscopically.

Despair, she decides
can take two forms.

The crying kind sustains the pain,
sears a pathway through the body
on an endless loop,
scouring burning
carving caverns
acid-etched by tears.

The cutting kind conveys a numbness,
a freedom as crimson blood flows
through smooth skin,
a flood of sweet relief
spreading through the body
a soothing fall.

Seen like that, she reasons,
she will choose cutting every time.

*More than a third of 16-25 year olds have self-harmed at some point
in their lives, when self-harm is defined as "someone intentionally
damaging or injuring their body." (Young Minds; 2018)*

Running

They've sent me to a therapist so I tell her stuff I think she wants to hear, the boring stuff; the way my teacher picks on me, how my best friend is a bitch behind my back, how my mum and dad never listen and how my little brother is a dick. She listens and she nods a lot, but doesn't ask too many questions, which is good. I start to tell her other stuff; the weirder stuff – how my body has to be in balance, the pressure on one side must be equal to the other, if I touch one thigh I must touch the other, if I step on pavement cracks with one foot I must do it with the other. I do this with my avatars, running on the screen, a shoulder broken on a boulder cancelled by a boulder to the other, a zigzag to the right followed by a zigzag to the left. I tell her how all my movements have a shadow, a constant stream of counting, how even when I'm talking to my friends there's another conversation in my head. She asks me if my life has any moments that are free of this? I tell her when I'm running, it's the only time I'm free. I can leap into a space that's only mine, I have the city to myself, a night-time place of space and freedom, no-one interrupts me here. I can forget the need to balance, I'm safe inside my perfect sphere. She tells me that it's time to finish, I tell her that I like her hair, which is true. I don't tell her I want to be a boy.

There was a 930% increase in referrals to the NHS Gender Identity Development Service between 2010 and 2016. (GIDS, 2016)

deluged

his eyes swim
vast blue seas
as his pain drowns him

his words flat
dead weighted
grief fathoms deep

he is sinking slowly
before my eyes
beyond my reach

surfacing for the third time
the loss he's swallowed
floods his face

take him to hospital
I tell his mother
don't let go

*The rate of suicide for young women under 25 increased by 83%
between 2012 and 2019, while the rate for young men rose by 25%.
(Office for National Statistics, 2019). While the numbers of
successful suicides are comparatively low, there has been a huge rise
in young people reporting having suicidal thoughts, especially since
the pandemic.*

Swallow

He's worried about his little sister.
She's called Swallow, a strange name
for a child but perhaps her parents tried to gift her
a soaring, swooping freedom she could never possess.
He's worried about his brother too, for different reasons.

His brother is a strutting-cock-of-the-walk sort of brother;
not like him, he's a plump-and-downy-clumsy sort of brother:
young together, free-wheeling flight was never in their sights
as they all huddled, feather-puffed, inside their fragile nest
as their parents sparred, quarrelsome and dangerous.

So when social workers came, attempting kindness
the *best interests of the children* the guiding light,
the three were rescued, but taken separately,
safer perhaps but lonely, a nest no longer
feathered with the old familiar scents.
And still he worries.

*The Children Act (1989) emphasises the need to place siblings
together "as far as is reasonably practicable". However, one of the
identified risk factors in that decision is the presence of sexual abuse
in the family.*

Stop

You fucker you fucker you fucker
you yell at me
as you barrel into the therapy room

black buzz-cut razoring your scalp,
you hurl the heavy wooden fire engine
across the floor

shut your mouth before I shut it for you
you scream in my face,
my lips pursed against your spittle.

Your father torched the house
with you inside, watching
for the fire engines to come.

No stop button –
you jab at the wooden toy –
emergency, emergency!

your soft-baby tummy protrudes
from your too-small dinosaur t-shirt:
he weed milk into my bottom.

you slump into a cushion
stare at me with vacant eyes –

don't matter if I hurt myself.

'Child sexual abuse has a profound effect that can last throughout adult life, leading to depression, post-traumatic stress disorder, self-harm and suicidality. It can severely impact the capacity to form trusting, loving and secure relationships.' (Independent Enquiry on Child Sexual Abuse, Interim Report, 2018)

Show and Tell

She scowls at me,
stands four-square
in her glasses and pink tights,
pulsing mistrust.

She grabs the dolls' house
choses the toys she wants to live inside,
turns her back on me.

Into the house she crams
mother and father doll,
four ragged children,
and a rowdy menagerie:
she makes the animals roam the house,
she locks the children in the garage.
The animals are fed and watered
with patience and tenderness,
the children are fed
with curses and threats.

She makes the mother doll fill her bedroom
with a king-sized bed, giant TV
and a shopping trolley
obscene with food.
It's my house
She makes the mother doll shout
I can have what I want.

The father doll unlocks the garage door,
seizes the smallest girl doll,
the one with the yellow plaits,
forces her legs apart.

She looks at me pointedly,
pauses the horror story of her play,
sits back –
Oh well
easy come, easy go
that's what my mum always says.

Official statistics on child sexual abuse are difficult to collect accurately as there is often a reluctance to disclose, and figures are therefore based on reported crime numbers only. However, in 2019, NSPCC and Childline services both reported a 12% increase in enquiries from the previous year, estimating that 1 in 20 children in the UK have been sexually abused. (NSPCC; 2019)

Orange

D'you like my new top?
I just bought it – orange
bright to cheer me up.
I've got no money to be fair
but this was only cheap.
My mum never notices
if I'm wearing something new.
She's off to Thailand soon
with her latest boyfriend, did I say?
Asked me if I'd be OK
She's worried about the cats
she's like, *you will look after them*
till I get back? I'll leave
some money for their food.
So I'll be alone again.
I told my dad,
and all he said was
She's really given up on parenting then.

So I was thinking, right
she's been like this for ages
she never really wanted kids
was never any good at it.
Didn't want to be with me
she told me that herself.
What I don't get is
why my dad left me with her
all that time ago?
He knew
what she was like.

So what I don't get is
why didn't anyone do
anything
all that time ago?
I only just thought this
it's – what'd they call it –
a light-bulb moment?
Not in a good way though.

What does it take to hold up the sky?

It wasn't easy, tightening the retaining ropes
judging the wind-speed, calibrating
for the possibility of hurricanes or tsunamis
while the storms raged for years.

You were rock-ribbed, determined
none should come to harm
and the sky held, soft-curled child,
but you did not

you buckled beneath a burden
too heavy for a slender frame,
folded into a blanket of shame
that should not belong to you.

Where did they go – the ones
who should have held up the sky?

Home Alone

Even when she's here
she's somewhere else –
yoga on a Goan beach,
sweat-wet Ibiza nights,
Copacabana fantasies,
ash falls from her cigarette
as she pours another drink.

I'm not in her head,
me – I'm on my own
self-stored in my room
gazing from the window.

Soon I'll go downstairs,
make my lunchbox, pack
a school-bag for tomorrow,
put out her smouldering stub,
pull the duvet over her on the sofa
and come back up to bed.

I have the pavement as my dreamland,
watching mercury puddles shudder
on a murky suburban street,
tensing at the urban foxy shriek,
listening to the slick–slick of tyres
as the night cruises home.

Me – I'm fine.

Callum v County Education Authority; [2018]; Court of Appeal.

There's a sound that's been following him around,
a low hum, moving with him like a force-field,
he loves the way it sends him surging into spaces
he hasn't been before, like opening an unknown door.
That day he went to Court, frisked and bag-checked, beckoned
forward by officials, no comforting sound was with him then,
only the hollow knocking of his fear. But oh, the glory of that place,
the soaring arches, sweeping staircases, marbled floors,
and patterns, patterns everywhere; and he, transported
in surprise: his mother muted by her tears,
her folder full of paperwork unread until his father said,
you tell them, son, what it's been like for you.
And then the humming started and the words poured out
in shapes he hardly knew, tracing the patterns of his truth;
how his teachers laughed when he read out loud, said
he'd never pass exams, how the other kids all yelled out *div*,
how he was labelled no matter what he did;
he opened up his life and he was heard.
Finding in his favour, the judge urged him
to believe there was no ceiling to his success.
The humming has been with him ever since, that low vibration
only he can hear; a cat's contented purr, or more like bees,
hive-busy, creating patterns, making vaulted halls
of sweetness, laying down supplies for the years ahead.

Approximately 80% of children placed in Special Education provision have dyslexia, often in combination with ADHD. A student with dyslexia is twice as likely to receive below Grade 4 in GCSE Maths and English. Approximately 50% of young people in Youth Offending institutes have dyslexia. (Report of the All Party Parliamentary Group; 2019)

Herding Words

They push against each other,
shove forwards, fighting
for his confused attention
why won't they stay still?
Just when he thinks he has them penned
they make a break for it
   spill out
      tumble
   escape
and he's lost again.

Stupid, that's what they spell.

Another try – calmer this time
a shape, a pattern, he has them now!
But as he goes to close the gate
      they leap
   scatter
      regroup
and turn to jeer.

Stupid, that's what he is.

His teacher calls him *dyslexic,*
disabled, more like
no-one gets As in this class.

Playground

At night he dreams of demons,
monsters that drive him
terrified to his parents' bed,
crying like the child
he hoped he had outgrown.

Try to forget
he tells himself
as each night approaches,
and if the demons don't come
it's not that he's outwitted them,
only that they've chosen
to lie in wait.

His days are a torment
of foreboding,
of caught breath
and clawed stomach,
the playground a place
where he is tossed
like a rabbit
by the baying hounds
of daylight.

*42% of children aged 10-15 years in England and Wales
experienced some form of bullying behaviour in the year ending
March 2020; 17% of those experienced cyber-bullying. (Office of
National Statistics, 2020.)*

dread

it's an existential crisis,
you tell me solemnly
as distress ripples
your thin skin
and your feet quiver

your name for the pain,
a way to explain it,
give yourself a lifeline
from the ocean trench
of despair

a tangle of dreadlocks
surrounds your face,
two delicate piercings
glisten
in your nose and lip

fragile umbilical cords
connecting you to yourself,
skin so thin it yields
to fear as a knife
glides through butter

Blindsided

Such a small grave boy
afro like a halo framing
his melancholy face.
His school bag sits on the floor
between us, burdensome.
We stare at it wordlessly.

He doesn't trust me – why should he?
I haven't lived his history,
will never know his skin.
He doesn't speak but silently
shreds tissues in his lap.

I give him pencil, paper, rubber
and he turns his back.
He draws carefully, small figures
that he doesn't let me see
erasing something that he hides,
thin grey filaments brushed
from the table top
falling to the floor.

We are falling away from one another,
too much unknown
too vast a sea, a country.
The shame of it is, just now
I'm what he has.

Eventually I ask if I can look –
tiny people, scurrying on the page
fat arms like wings, all bearing guns.
Angels with guns? I ask, confused.
No, AK47s, he corrects.
He slumps forward, head on arms –

I'm tired of being black.

BAME children make up 16% of looked-after children, and more than half of young people in custody are from a BAME group. (Government Youth Justice Statistics; 2021)

Thirteen

It was that birthday card that did it....
that card from my Nan
she should never of sent it
they're not supposed to contact me
but they wrote in it
We'll always love you - Mum and Dad
or some shit like that
so I opened the card
and it shocked me, right,
took me back
and I went to the cloakroom
and that girl was there –
she's a bit special, a bit ASD
you know what I mean
they say I raped her, so I suppose I did
but I don't remember – just blank
always love me – what does that mean?
touched me, fingered me more like
and the rest
sick.
Not my real dad anyway
he fucked off when I was born
never seen him
his name's Steve I think – drives a lorry
not much to go on
she didn't choose well, my mum
fucking bitch
so what'll happen now?
suppose they'll move me again...
thirteen – not much of a birthday, was it?
not much of a life is it?
life's a bitch and then you marry one
that's what they say
if I get that far.

Complex PTSD can arise from on-going childhood abuse, especially if the perpetrator is a close relative. It can give rise to flashbacks, intense anger, shame and dissociation. The original trauma can be retriggered by unexpected events. (Mind; 2021)
31% of children in care have had three or more placement moves within a year, exactly the same proportion that are moved with less than 24 hours notice. (NSPCC, 2018)

Shame

It's not fair, I'm too young for this,
this happens to old people, not to me.
I feel ashamed of him, awful, but it's true.
He had a stroke, didn't he,
my dad, only forty-three.
And now he can't do anything,
can't walk, can't talk, can't be my dad.
I can't bear to look at him. Sometimes
I wish he'd died – how bad is that?
He used to have a laugh, a muck-about,
now he's in a wheel-chair,
dribbles when he eats –
it's horrible, he's horrible
and so am I.
Best I can do is play this game –
poke him to see if he can feel.
He smiles if he does.
He wanted to come to parent's evening
in his wheelchair last week. I said no,
made up some lie, imagine if he did!
I couldn't bear it, all my friends
feeling sorry for me,
saying stuff.
The Head told the whole school
when I was off. Shamed or what.
It's the pity that's the worst.
It's my mum I really hate.
I mean my dad can't help it, right,
I know I shouldn't say it but
he's like a sort of imbecile –
I know it's not his fault.
But my mum, she's had enough,
she wants out I think,
says this isn't how she imagined life would be.
I found this dating app on her phone –
probably shouldn't have looked,
but there you go.

Called her out on it, she screamed at me,
then, the weirdest thing,
she gave me her wedding ring.
I mean, what's that about?
I don't want to be married
to my dad, that's her job.
I don't want to look after him,
I'm too young for that.

Cygnet

I watch her as she comes
step-dragging down the path
sullen, sulky
her feet betray her
meeting me was never her idea.

This will be hard, I think
and so it proves,
blood from a stone girl,
her words betray her
talking to me was never her idea.

She draws blood
from white limbs
with a pencil sharpener blade,
this is her idea
a pressure-letting
to ease numb pain
taut as drumskin.

From a thicket of hair
she rolls her eyes,
flashes me a glimpse
of the woman she will become,
she rolls her eyes
and rolls herself alive

brave as a swan
in full sail, gathering
her freedom to her like a song
that one day will be glorious
but today is muted,
muffled by grey down
waiting to be shed.

Coat

She peeps out from a shroud
of ink-black hair, picking
at her fingertips, her plucking
shreds the fragile air between us
as she waits for me to help.

Her father died when she was six,
drinking too much
not loving her enough
to see her grow: sixteen now
she has grown careless with herself.

She tells me how each week her father
used to take her to the local baths,
he would watch her swim
and in the park he'd hold her coat
while she went on the swings.

One day they left her small red coat behind,
forgotten on a seat, he remembered
and went back for it, a simple act:
he will never know she keeps it still
hidden carefully amongst her things.

*Up to 40% of bereaved children still show disturbance two years
after the bereavement. Longing for reunion is common and may
lead to serious suicidal thoughts. There is a five-fold increase in
childhood psychiatric disorders in this group. (British Medical
Journal, 1998)*

puppies

all quiet morning
   no-one up except the sun
and you, tiptoeing

softly down the stairs
   to see the new arrivals
young, unguarded

commas of blind helplessness
   blanket-snuggled
curled and breathing

warm-milk-and-biscuit smell
   squirm of innocence
finger-soft and yielding

your fingers squeeze
   the smoothness
pinion tiny limbs

so trusting
   you could do anything
like he did to you

When she was four...

and had learnt to pedal, she was off, freewheeling down
    the careless lanes of childhood, no backward glance

she whizzed her way through small school, waving to friends
    while swinging around corners at tremendous speed

a swerve and wobble as she reached thirteen, those friends
    not always what they seemed and the lane home longer

she didn't know her cautious parents never took the stabilisers off
    just in case of accidents they had anxiously agreed

so she never learnt to balance, although she thought she could
    and as roads became more crowded and the potholes grew

her small wheels fell away and she was balancing unaided
    but she looked back, and as adulthood overtook her

the ordinary stuff of grown-up life rolled past – a failed romance
    an unrewarding job, an illness – and she wavered

unpractised as she was, she panicked and toppled sideways,
    lying in the gutter she thought of giving up

but she still longed for perfect balance and she practised
    and she practised until her knees were sore

now at twenty-four, she is mistress of her balance and rides a unicycle,
    waving to the astonished crowds as she cruises into life.

"And the end of all our exploring
Will be to arrive where we started
And to know the place for the first time."

T.S.Eliot (*Little Gidding*)

Acknowledgements

I would like to thank the editors of the following publications and websites where these poems were first published:

'Mouth Organ' was published in *Eighty Four* (Verve Poetry Press, 2019)

'Home Alone' was published on-line by *Nine Muses*, 2018, and was a Best of the Net nominee.

'Cygnet' was commended in The Hippocrates Prize, 2021, and published in *The Hippocrates Prize Anthology*, 2021

'Callum v Local Education Authority' and 'The Art of Disappearance' were published in *Bridges*, Newcastle University, 2019 and 2018 respectively.

I would also like to thank my tutors at the Poetry School, and especially Tammy Yoseloff for her unfailing support; the members of the Canada Water Poetry Group; the Tercet group, (you know who you are!), the members of the Mid-Kent Stanza Group, and my psychotherapy peer supervision group.

Also grateful thanks for all their love and support go to my family, Edmund, Rafe and Annie, and also to friends and neighbours Ruth and Gerry, who have offered supper and encouragement throughout lockdown. To Janice and Dónall for publishing these poems; and most importantly, to all the children I have had the privilege of knowing.

Diana Cant
2021

Diana Cant is a Consultant Child and Adolescent Psychotherapist who has worked for many years with highly distressed and depressed young people, some of whom have been severely abused and are often in residential care. She now offers consultation and supervision to fellow professionals. She won the inaugural Child Psychotherapy Essay Prize, has written many articles and professional papers, and contributed to mental health programmes on BBC 4.

She has an MA in Poetry Writing from Newcastle University through the Poetry School in London. She is a member of the Mid Kent Stanza Group, and the Canada Water Poetry Group. Her work has been published in *Finished Creatures*, *The Alchemy Spoon*, *Brittle Star*, *Ink, Sweat and Tears*, and *Nine Muses*. Her poetry has also appeared in various anthologies, such as *Humanagerie*, *Eighty Four*, *Places of Poetry* and *Beyond the Storm*. She was longlisted in the Ginko Prize, 2019, and commended in the Hippocrates Prize, the Ver, and the Plough prizes in 2021. Her pamphlet, *Student Bodies 1968,* was published by Clayhanger Press in 2020. She lives and works in rural Kent.